IN THE BEGINNG

A Creation Story

Mike Charron

In The Beginning: A Creation Story Copyright © 2019 InHisImage Publishing. All Rights Reserved.

In the BEGINNING

God created the HEAVENS and the EARTH

The earth was formless and void

And DARKNESS

Was over the

SURFACE

of the

ABYSS

Rev 20:3   Luk 8:31   Rev 17:8

The

SPIRIT OF GOD

was moving over the

SURFACE

of the

WATERS

Then God said

Let the WATERS teem with swarms

Of living creatures

Matt 13:47-49

And the LESSER to govern the night

He made the STARS also

Matt 27:45   Matt 5:14

And there was evening and there was morning

A

THIRD
DAY

Matt 13:31-32

Matt 13:31-32

Then God created man in

HIS OWN IMAGE

And He said

Be fruitfull and multiply

Fill the EARTH

And subdue it

Matt 13:31-32

Rule over the FISH of the sea

The BIRDS of the HEAVENS

And over every living thing

That moves on the EARTH

Rom 8:29　　　　Mark 8:24-25　　　　Matt 16:24

Thus the HEAVENS

And the EARTH

Were completed

And ALL their HOSTS

God completed ALL His work

And He rested

Rev 21:1

www.ingramcontent.com/pod-product-compliance
Lightning Source LLC
Chambersburg PA
CBHW042018090526
44589CB00024B/2838